CONTENTS

Introduction

CHAPTER 1: A brief history of blockchain

CHAPTER 2: How Blockchain Work: The Basic

CHAPTER 3: Why Blockchain Is Safe

CHAPTER 4: Uses of Blockchain

CHAPTER 5: Blockchain and Cryptocurrency: An Overview

CHAPTER 6: The Future of Blockchain

CHAPTER 7: FAQs and Misconceptions about Blockchain

CHAPTER 8: How To Get Started With Blockchain

Conclusion

Appendix

INTRODUCTION

Think of blockchain as a special kind of digital ledger or record book. Imagine a physical notebook where every page records different transactions. Now, imagine that this notebook is not kept by one person but shared among thousands, maybe millions, of people. Every time someone writes something in it, every other person gets the same update. This way, no one can change what's written after the fact, and everyone can see what's in the notebook at any time.

Blockchain works similarly. It's a system that securely records transactions (like payments or exchanges of information) across many computers at once. Each transaction is stored in a "block," and these blocks are connected in a sequence (or "chain"). This creates a long, unchangeable chain of records — hence the name "blockchain."

Why Should Seniors Care About Blockchain?

Now, you might be wondering, why should I care about this new technology? Well, blockchain has the potential to change the way we live and do things, much like the internet did years ago. It could make things like managing your personal finances, buying items online, and even accessing medical records much safer and faster.

Even though blockchain may seem complicated at first, its core purpose is simple: to keep records in a way that makes them secure and almost impossible to alter. Once something is recorded, it's locked in and shared with everyone else in the system. This means you can trust that it's accurate and hasn't been tampered with.

The Benefits of Blockchain Technology

Here are a few reasons why blockchain technology is gaining attention around the world:

Security: Since blockchain records are stored across many computers, it's almost impossible for hackers to alter the data. This makes it a very secure way to store and transfer information.

Transparency: Everyone who's part of the blockchain network can see the same information. This openness ensures trust between users.

Decentralization: Unlike a traditional system controlled by one central entity (like a bank or government), blockchain is decentralized, meaning no one person or organization controls it. This reduces the risk of manipulation or corruption.

Efficiency: Blockchain can make processes like transferring money or signing contracts quicker, cutting out the need for middlemen like banks or lawyers.

CHAPTER ONE

A Brief History of Blockchain.

Blockchain has been around for over a decade, but many people, especially seniors, are still unfamiliar with what it is and how it works. The good news is that it's easier to understand than it seems! This book will walk you through the basics, one step at a time.

Origins of Blockchain

Blockchain technology was first introduced in 2008 by someone (or a group of people) using the pseudonym "Satoshi Nakamoto." Satoshi's goal was to create a system for people to send and receive money without needing a middleman, like a bank. This idea led to the creation of **Bitcoin**, the first and most famous cryptocurrency.

Before Bitcoin, people had to rely on banks or other financial institutions to process transactions, especially online. This reliance on third parties meant that you needed to trust these institutions to handle your money securely and fairly. But Satoshi's blockchain technology changed that by allowing people to deal directly with each other without needing to go through a bank.

How Blockchain Has Evolved Over Time

Since the creation of Bitcoin, blockchain technology has expanded far beyond just digital currencies. Today, many industries are exploring how blockchain can help them do things more efficiently and securely. For example:

Healthcare: Hospitals and clinics can use blockchain to store patient records in a way that keeps them safe and private but still allows doctors and nurses to access them when needed.

Finance: Banks are looking into using blockchain to speed up money transfers and reduce the cost of doing business.

Voting: Governments are researching how blockchain could make elections more secure and transparent.

What started as an idea for creating a digital currency has become a technology with many uses and potential to reshape how we do things in everyday life.

CHAPTER TWO

How Blockchain Works: The Basics

To understand blockchain, let's first talk about what a "block" is. A block is a digital piece of information that holds transaction data, like the details of a money transfer. Each block is connected to the previous one, forming a chain. This chain of blocks is called the blockchain.

Blocks and Chains: A Simple Explanation

Now that you have an idea of what blockchain is, let's talk about how it actually works.

Imagine you and a group of friends decide to play a game where everyone takes turns writing down what they did during the day on a shared piece of paper. Every time someone writes something, the paper gets passed to the next person, and no one is allowed to erase anything that's already written. Eventually, this paper will be filled with information from everyone, and no one can change what's been recorded.

In blockchain, this "paper" is the block, and once it's full of information (usually transactions), it gets sealed and added to a chain of other blocks. This chain of blocks — or "blockchain" — becomes a permanent record of all transactions. Each block contains a unique code (like a fingerprint), the details of the transactions, and a link to the previous block, which keeps the chain secure.

How Transactions Are Verified

In a traditional system, a bank verifies if you have enough money in your account when you make a payment. In a blockchain, there's no need for a central authority like a bank to do this. Instead, computers around the world (called "nodes") check and verify transactions.

Here's how it works:

When you send money to someone using a blockchain system, that transaction is sent to the network of nodes.

The nodes check to make sure the transaction is legitimate. For example, they make sure you actually have the money you're trying to send.

Once enough nodes agree that the transaction is valid, it gets added to a new block.

The block is then added to the blockchain, where it will remain permanently.

The Role of Cryptography

Cryptography is a method of protecting information through complex mathematical techniques. In the blockchain, cryptography helps keep transactions safe. Each block is linked to the previous one using cryptography, which ensures that no one can change a block once it's been added to the chain.

The use of cryptography means that only the intended parties can see or access the details of the transactions, while everyone else can still verify that the transaction happened.

CHAPTER THREE

Why Blockchain Is Safe

One of the main reasons people trust blockchain is because of how it's designed. Unlike traditional databases, blockchain is decentralized, which means there is no single company or person in control of it. This makes it much harder for hackers to break into.

Decentralization: What It Means and Why It's Important

One of the biggest reasons why blockchain is so safe is because it's decentralized. In traditional systems, you usually have one company or person in charge of managing data. For example, your bank controls your financial records. This makes the system vulnerable if that one central entity is hacked or makes a mistake.

Blockchain operates differently. Instead of relying on one central authority, blockchain distributes the data across a network of computers (nodes). This means that even if one part of the network is compromised, the rest of the system remains secure.

Think of it like storing important documents in multiple places. If one storage location is damaged, the documents stored in the other places remain safe.

Public vs. Private Blockchains

There are two main types of blockchains: public and private.

Public blockchains: Anyone can join the network and participate in verifying transactions. Bitcoin is an example of a public blockchain.

Private blockchains: Only certain people or organizations are allowed to participate. This type of blockchain is often used by businesses for specific purposes.

Both types of blockchains use cryptography to ensure that data is secure, but private blockchains tend to be used in situations where more control is needed over who can access the network.

The Role of Miners and Nodes

In some blockchains, like Bitcoin, the process of verifying transactions is done by "miners." These miners use powerful computers to solve complex math problems, which helps confirm the transaction and add it to the blockchain. In return for their work, miners are rewarded with cryptocurrency (like Bitcoin) Nodes, on the other hand, are computers that help maintain the blockchain by storing a copy of the entire blockchain and verifying transactions. While not all nodes are miners, all miners are nodes.

CHAPTER FOUR

Uses of Blockchain

Most people know blockchain because of cryptocurrency, but the technology can be used in many other areas as well. For example, hospitals can use blockchain to securely store patient information, and banks can use it to speed up transactions.

Most people associate blockchain with cryptocurrencies like Bitcoin, but the technology has many other applications that can make everyday life easier and more secure. In this chapter, we'll explore some practical uses of blockchain that are relevant to different industries and services.

Cryptocurrency: The Best-Known Application

The most famous use of blockchain is cryptocurrency. Bitcoin was the first cryptocurrency, and it uses blockchain to enable secure, peer-to-peer money transfers. Unlike traditional currencies that are controlled by banks or governments, cryptocurrencies are decentralized, meaning they aren't controlled by any single entity.

Some examples of popular cryptocurrencies include:

Bitcoin: The original and most well-known cryptocurrency.

Ethereum: Another widely used cryptocurrency, which also allows people to build apps on its blockchain.

Litecoin: Known for its faster transaction times compared to Bitcoin.

Cryptocurrencies allow people to send money anywhere in the world quickly and often with lower fees than traditional banks. However, the value of cryptocurrencies can be volatile, meaning their prices can go up or down quickly.

How Blockchain Can Be Used in Healthcare, Finance, and Other Industries

Blockchain technology can be used for far more than just digital currencies. Here are some examples of how different industries are using it:

Healthcare:

Medical Records: Blockchain can securely store patients' medical records, making sure that they are accurate and can't be altered. This helps doctors and hospitals access important health information quickly while keeping it private and secure.

Supply Chains for Medicine: Blockchain can track the journey of medicines from the manufacturer to the pharmacy, ensuring that medications are authentic and not counterfeit.

Finance:

Faster Payments: Blockchain can make international money transfers faster and cheaper. Traditional banks often take days to process international payments, but blockchain can do it in minutes or hours.

Smart Contracts: These are contracts that automatically execute themselves when certain conditions are met. For example, a smart contract might release payment when a product is delivered. This can reduce the need for lawyers or middlemen.

Real Estate:

Property Transfers: Blockchain can streamline the process of buying and selling property. By recording property ownership and transfers on the blockchain, the need for extensive paperwork is reduced, and transactions can be completed more quickly.

Voting:
Secure Elections: Blockchain could be used to create secure, transparent voting systems. Since the blockchain is tamper-proof, it can ensure that votes are accurately counted and that no one can alter the results.

Supply Chain Management:
Tracking Goods: Businesses can use blockchain to track the movement of goods from the manufacturer to the store. This makes it easier to ensure that products are authentic and haven't been tampered with along the way.

Real-World Examples
Walmart: The retail giant is using blockchain to track the origins of food products. This helps them quickly trace the source of any contamination during food safety investigations.

IBM and Maersk: These companies are using blockchain to track shipping containers, making the process of moving goods across borders more efficient.

As you can see, blockchain is being used in a wide range of industries to improve security, transparency, and efficiency. While we may not see these applications in our daily lives yet, blockchain is steadily making its way into more and more aspects of modern life.

CHAPTER FIVE

Blockchain technology made cryptocurrencies like Bitcoin possible. In this chapter, we will explain the differences between the most popular cryptocurrencies and how seniors can safely engage with them if they are interested.

Blockchain and Cryptocurrency: An Overview
While blockchain is the technology that powers cryptocurrency, it's important to understand how the two are connected, yet distinct. In this chapter, we'll look deeper into what cryptocurrency is and how seniors can engage with it safely.

What is Cryptocurrency?

Cryptocurrency is digital money that operates on a blockchain network. Instead of relying on banks or governments to verify transactions, cryptocurrencies use blockchain's decentralized system to make sure that money can be transferred securely.

Just like traditional money, cryptocurrencies can be used to buy goods and services, although they aren't accepted everywhere yet. Some online stores, travel companies, and even some retail outlets accept cryptocurrency as payment.

What makes cryptocurrency different from regular money is that it's digital, meaning it exists only on the internet. You can't hold a Bitcoin in your hand like a dollar bill, but you can store it securely in a digital wallet, which you can access from your computer or a smart phone.

Bitcoin vs. Other Cryptocurrencies

While Bitcoin is the most well-known cryptocurrency, there are thousands of others. Some of them serve different purposes:

Ethereum: In addition to being a digital currency, Ethereum allows people to create decentralized apps (or "dapps") and smart contracts on its blockchain.

Ripple (XRP): Designed for fast international money transfers, Ripple is used by some banks and financial institutions.

Litecoin: Similar to Bitcoin, but with faster transaction times and lower fees.

Each cryptocurrency has its unique features, and choosing the right one depends on what you plan to use it for.

How to Safely Buy and Store Cryptocurrency

If you're thinking about buying cryptocurrency, it's important to know how to do it safely. Here are a few steps to get started:

Choose a Reliable Platform:

You'll need to use an exchange to buy cryptocurrency. Some popular and trusted platforms include Coinbase, Binance, and Kraken. Always make sure the platform is secure and reputable before signing up.

Set Up a Digital Wallet:

A digital wallet is where you store your cryptocurrency. Some wallets are software that you can install on your phone or computer, while others are physical devices (called "hardware wallets") that look like USB drives. Hardware wallets are generally considered more secure because they store your cryptocurrency offline, away from hackers.

Enable Security Features:

Always enable two-factor authentication (2FA) on your exchange account and wallet to add an extra layer of security. This means that even if someone gets your password, they can't access your account without also having access to your phone or email.

Be Cautious of Scams:

Unfortunately, there are scams in the cryptocurrency world. Never share your wallet's private keys (the codes that let you access your cryptocurrency), and be wary of any "too good to be true" investment offers.

For seniors, cryptocurrency can be an interesting way to explore new forms of digital finance, but it's crucial to do so cautiously and with an understanding of the risks involved.

CHAPTER SIX

The Future of Blockchain

Blockchain is still evolving, and many experts believe it will change how businesses and governments operate in the future. Seniors, in particular, could benefit from blockchain in areas like health care and personal finance.

Blockchain technology is still relatively new, and its full potential is only beginning to be understood. In this chapter, we'll explore what the future may hold for blockchain and how it could impact seniors in particular.

Trends in Blockchain Technology

Here are some trends that are likely to shape the future of blockchain:

More Applications Beyond Cryptocurrency:
As we've discussed, blockchain is already being used in industries like healthcare, finance, and supply chain management. In the future, we'll see even more industries adopting blockchain to improve their operations, from education to entertainment.

Wider Use of Smart Contracts:
Smart contracts are digital agreements that automatically execute when certain conditions are met. In the future, they could be used to simplify many legal processes, such as estate planning, by ensuring that everything is handled according to the agreed terms without needing a lawyer to intervene.

Integration with the Internet of Things (IoT):
The Internet of Things refers to everyday objects (like appliances, cars, or even medical devices) that are connected to the internet. Blockchain could be used to manage data between these devices, creating a more secure and efficient way for them to communicate.

Greater Transparency in Government and Voting:
Governments may use blockchain to ensure more transparent elections and public records, making it harder for fraud or corruption to occur.

How Seniors Can Benefit from Blockchain in the Future
Blockchain could bring many benefits to seniors, especially in areas like:

Healthcare: With more control over their medical records, seniors could have better access to their health data and share it easily with doctors.

Estate Planning and Wills: Smart contracts could simplify the process of managing wills and estates, ensuring that everything is handled according to the individual's wishes.

Identity Protection: Blockchain's security features could help protect seniors from identity theft and fraud, which are major concerns for older adults.While blockchain may still seem like a new and unfamiliar technology, it has the potential to improve many aspects of life in the future.

CHAPTER SEVEN

FAQs and Misconceptions About Blockchain

In this chapter, we'll address common questions seniors have, like "Is blockchain only for tech experts?" or "Is it too late for me to learn?"

Many people, especially seniors, have questions and doubts when they first hear about blockchain. It's a new concept for most, so it's perfectly normal to feel uncertain. In this chapter, we'll address some of the most common questions and misconceptions to help you feel more comfortable with the idea of blockchain.

Common Questions Seniors Have About Blockchain
Is blockchain only for young, tech-savvy people?
Absolutely not! While younger generations may seem to adopt new technologies faster, blockchain is designed to be used by anyone. Once you understand the basics, it's no more complicated than using a smartphone or navigating the internet.

Can I trust blockchain with my personal information?
Blockchain is one of the most secure technologies available today because it uses encryption and decentralization. While no system is 100% foolproof, blockchain's structure makes it extremely difficult for hackers to alter information once it's been recorded. That said, always be cautious when sharing personal information online and use secure services.

Do I need to invest in cryptocurrency to use blockchain?
Not at all. While cryptocurrency is one application of blockchain, there are many other uses. You don't need to invest in or buy cryptocurrency to benefit from blockchain technology. Many companies and industries are exploring how blockchain can be used to improve services, from healthcare to voting.

Is it too late for me to learn about blockchain?
It's never too late to learn something new! Blockchain technology is still evolving, and understanding it now can help you stay informed about future developments that may affect your daily life.

Debunking Popular Myths

Myth: Blockchain is just a fad that will go away.
Reality: While blockchain is still a relatively new technology, it's gaining traction in many industries due to its security, transparency, and efficiency. The technology is likely to be around for a long time and will play a bigger role in our lives in the future.

Myth: Blockchain is used mainly for illegal activities.
Reality: Like any technology, blockchain can be used for both good and bad purposes. However, the vast majority of blockchain use is legal and focused on improving things like finance, healthcare, and supply chain management. Governments and companies are increasingly adopting blockchain to enhance security and efficiency.

Myth: Blockchain is too complex for the average person.
Reality: While the technology behind blockchain can be complex, understanding how to use it doesn't have to be. Just like you don't need to understand the inner workings of a car engine to drive a car, you don't need to be a tech expert to benefit from blockchain.

CHAPTER EIGHT

How to Get Started with Blockchain

For seniors who want to start learning more or even engage with blockchain technology, this chapter provides simple, step-by-step instructions and trusted resources to continue their journey.

This structure, expanded with detailed, simplified explanations and analogies, would form an approximately 50-page ebook. Would you like me to begin fleshing out specific chapters or refine any sections first? Sure! Let's start expanding the chapters, making sure to keep the explanations simple, using analogies and everyday language that seniors can easily relate to. Here's the expanded version of the first few chapters:

By now, you have a good understanding of what blockchain is, how it works, and how it's being used in the world today. If you're interested in exploring blockchain further, there are simple ways to get started, even if you're new to the technology. This chapter will guide you through the basics of getting involved with blockchain, step by step.

Simple Steps for Seniors to Engage with Blockchain

Learn the Basics First

Before diving in, take some time to learn more about blockchain and cryptocurrency through trusted sources. There are many online courses and videos designed specifically for beginners. Websites like Coursera, Khan Academy, and even YouTube have easy-to-follow lessons that can help you get a solid foundation.

Join a Blockchain Community

There are online forums and communities where people discuss blockchain technology. Websites like Reddit (r/cryptocurrency and r/blockchain) and other tech forums can be good places to ask questions and learn from others who are interested in blockchain. You'll find that many people are happy to help beginners.

Start Small with Cryptocurrency

If you want to experiment with cryptocurrency, consider starting with a small amount. You don't need to invest a lot of money — just a few dollars' worth of cryptocurrency is enough to get started. You can use trusted platforms like Coinbase or Binance to buy and sell cryptocurrency securely.

Use a Digital Wallet

As mentioned in an earlier chapter, you'll need a digital wallet to store your cryptocurrency. Start by using a software wallet, which is an app you can download to your phone or computer. Make sure to enable security features like two-factor authentication (2FA) to protect your wallet.

Practice Caution

Be wary of scams. Unfortunately, there are bad actors out there who prey on newcomers to the world of blockchain and cryptocurrency. Never give out your wallet's private key, and avoid investment opportunities that promise guaranteed returns — these are often scams.

Experiment with Blockchain Apps

Beyond cryptocurrency, there are many blockchain-based apps (called decentralized apps or "dApps") that you can explore. Some dApps focus on gaming, while others offer secure messaging or social networking services. Trying out a few dApps can give you a feel for how blockchain is being used in everyday life.

Resources for Learning More About Blockchain

Here are some resources to help you continue your journey with blockchain:

Coursera (www.coursera.org): Offers beginner-friendly courses on blockchain and cryptocurrency.

Khan Academy (www.khanacademy.org): Provides educational videos on a variety of topics, including blockchain.

Coinbase Learn (www.coinbase.com/learn): A resource for beginners to understand cryptocurrency and blockchain, provided by a major cryptocurrency exchange.

Reddit (www.reddit.com): A platform where you can join discussions about blockchain and cryptocurrency in various forums like r/blockchain or r/cryptocurrency.

By starting with these resources, you'll gradually become more familiar with blockchain and feel more confident exploring its many uses.

CONCLUSION

Blockchain technology may seem complex at first, but with a bit of patience and curiosity, anyone can understand and even benefit from it. Much like the internet, blockchain is poised to become a part of our everyday lives, bringing

improvements in security, transparency, and efficiency to many industries.

As seniors, embracing this new technology can open doors to exciting opportunities, from better managing personal finances to ensuring more secure

healthcare records. By learning about blockchain today, you're preparing yourself for the future and gaining valuable knowledge that can enhance your life.

Whether you decide to invest in cryptocurrency or simply want to understand

how blockchain works, the key is to keep learning and exploring. Technology can be a great tool when used wisely, and blockchain is no exception.

Thank you for taking the time to read this guide. We hope you feel more confident about what blockchain is, how it works, and how it can fit into your life. The future is bright, and blockchain is just one piece of the puzzle that will shape how we live in the digital age.

APPENDIX

Glossary of Key Terms

Blockchain: A digital ledger that records transactions across many computers, making the information secure and hard to alter.

Cryptocurrency: A form of digital money that uses blockchain technology to operate without the need for banks or governments.

Bitcoin: The first and most popular cryptocurrency, created in 2008 by an unknown person or group called Satoshi Nakamoto.

Ethereum: A cryptocurrency that also allows developers to build decentralized applications (dApps) on its blockchain.

Decentralization: A system in which control is spread out over many locations or participants rather than being controlled by one central entity.

Digital Wallet: A software or hardware tool that allows you to store and manage cryptocurrency.

Smart Contract: A digital contract that automatically executes when certain conditions are met, eliminating the need for middlemen.

Node: A computer in the blockchain network that helps verify transactions and store copies of the blockchain.

Mining: The process of verifying transactions on a blockchain, often rewarded with cryptocurrency like Bitcoin.

DISCLAIMER

This book was written and assisted using artificial intelligence (AI). While efforts were made to ensure accuracy, the content is for informational and educational purposes only.
The author and AI tools do not guarantee its completeness or accuracy and are not liable for errors. Readers should independently verify any information.

Thanks for reading.

www.ingramcontent.com/pod-product-compliance
Lightning Source LLC
Chambersburg PA
CBHW071000220526
45471CB00007B/3110